ISBN 978-0-484-14912-9
PIBN 10159011

HEAD-CULTURE AND HEART-CULTURE;

OR, THE

ELEMENTARY EDUCATION ACT

DISSECTED.

BY

CHRISTIAN PLAYFAIR.

.... " we forget
To pay ourselves, what to ourselves is debt."

Oxford and London:

JAMES PARKER AND CO.

1874.

NOTICE.

THE bulk of this Pamphlet was written last autumn, before there was any prospect either of a general Election, or of a change of Ministry. It was laid aside for a time owing to those circumstances, and has since been delayed coming out for want of leisure.

CONTENTS.

HEAD-CULTURE AND HEART-CULTURE, &c.

CHAPTER I.

THE world is going mad upon intellect. One of our greatest living theologians has occupied his declining years in compiling a 'grammar of assent'—observe, not of faith—as a panacea for scepticism; and one of our greatest living statesmen but the other day plumed himself on having invented a scheme for educating the masses in everything else but religion as a panacea for crime. Numbers have been sent to Bedlam again and again for aberrations of mind infinitely less serious in their consequences. Two Mephistophiles, acting in concert, could not have schemed more profoundly to send us all back to the woods. I am far from insinuating that either of them at all schemed with that object in view, or that both together have schemed alone. We are most of us bound hand-and-foot to the age in which we live: and the age in which we live, far from being a creative power, is bound hand-and-foot to the problems that were being discussed when it was young; to questions that had descended to it from former ages but half solved. Not one in a million of those whose boast it is to lead public opinion is an original thinker. Nobody can lead public opinion who is not a plagiarist, *malgré lui.* He must cater for the public, or he will not find hearers: he must speak to them in a language that they can understand, and deal with ideas with which they are familiar from childhood: he must talk to them of what they are thinking and interested about most. They won't bear to be merely set thinking on what he may deem of importance; they will insist on his telling them their thoughts, aye, and on his making the best of them that he can. All our leading men are leading men in proportion as they are plagiarists and time-servers: they can never venture to think for themselves: they must think as others think, and for others. As to creating public thought, they know they might as well attempt raising the wind; the exercise of their highest talents lies in anticipating it; and the longer this is done beforehand, the greater their fame. Many, doubtless, have started with aspirations of their own when they were young, but they soon found that swimming against the stream was a thankless task; and the moment they got into tidal waters, they had enough to do to keep themselves floating. Henceforward they were borne pell-mell on waves of thought that had been gathering for centuries, or by the ground-swell of successive convulsions of the ocean ages ago.

If "birds of a feather flock together," it is also true that "extremes meet;" and extremes not merely meet, but are sometimes as nearly related as parent and child. As I walk about Oxford, and see nine-tenths of the students I meet habited in some fantastic dress, without which it would be heresy to maintain that cricket, boating, or foot-ball, *et hoc genus omne*, yclept athletic sports, can be played now; it has always struck me that if I analyzed their features, and attempted to trace their pedigree from their general tone, I should be driven to the conclusion that I remembered their grandsire living in seclusion at Littlemore, though nobody would have taken him for a possible ancestor of muscular Christians then. Similarly, when I turn into the colleges, and enquire what the discipline, and what the lectures are, and what is taken up ordinarily for the schools now, I find my thoughts, in spite of myself, reverting to the Elementary Education Act of 1870. Here the paternity may be reversed, but the affinity is a matter of fact no less. The man of the future, the generation that is to step into our shoes when our heads are low, enters upon life with all the finish that competitive examinations and athletic sports can impart to mind and muscle: and according to his certificates of mind and muscle he has been taught from childhood to expect he must stand or fall, prosper or fail. If he can excel in both so much the better; and if his muscles are powerful, even if his mind is deficient, his case is not hopeless; but, without mind or muscle, he may as well retire from the struggle; he has nothing else to fall back upon; there is nothing in him besides these worth a rush.

The worship of intellect and the worship of Priapus are correlatives; in other words, one naturally suggests the other; and they who are foremost in intellectualising religion, and secularising education, will have to answer to posterity for both. There may be, possibly, more refinement in the worship of the head than of the heel; and there may be magic in the word "progress;" but as nine-tenths of us come into the world blessed with more brawn than brain, the worship of the head is never likely to become catholic, and the worship of the heel is already recommencing among the musculars. It may be that we are some way off yet from our destination; but that we are nearing it, must be patent to all. It is brought home to us in a hundred ways. We find evidences of it in the columns of every daily paper. I confine myself to the news of this country. I might confine myself to the columns of the "Times" for the last two months of the year past. When it is vacation time, people are apt to be more frank and outspoken in what they say. When the now Prime Minister was installed Lord Rector at Glasgow last autumn, passing over all the honied amenities that distilled from his lips, which it might be difficult, and certainly would take long to gauge, let us attend only to what was stated by the staid sententious Scotchman presiding over that University in concluding his reply to them:—

"I believe," said he, "that the motive which has mainly

influenced the students of the University to elect him as
their academic chief, is one the force of which men of all
shades of political opinion must feel, and one which as we
contemplate his career as a statesman and a man of letters,
unites all of us, Whig, Tory, or Radical, in this brilliant
assembly, in an admiration of *intellectual power*, and of
that greatness, which *only intellectual power* can worthily
achieve[a]."

We are not told whether this sentiment elicited "marks
of adhesion" or not; but we may not doubt its having been
accepted unhesitatingly, and endorsed unanimously, by the
vast audience to whom it was addressed. We may not
doubt; for what is it, in fact, but the principle on which
every Fellowship and most Scholarships at Oxford and Cam-
bridge are now filled; on which competitive examinations
have been decreed for most branches of the public ser-
vice; and success in every competitive examination depends? Money is the only qualification capable now of
gaining a hearing or making a stand against intellect.
Everything else goes to the wall. If this is not intellect-
worship, and if intellect-worship is not creature-worship,
I know not what is.

Look again at the exhibition of taste, to which the general
public was admitted in Westminster Abbey just a fortnight
later. Its Ordinary, whose duty consists in upholding the
law, and in doing his utmost at all times to prevent any
possible breach of the law in that place—to say no more—
took advantage of a day set apart by the authorities of the
Church for purely Church purposes, to shew his respect for
the laws of the realm as well as of the Church, by setting
them both at defiance; and inviting English Churchmen to
come and hear their religion contrasted unfavourably with
other religions by a layman and a foreigner, in preference
to the sermon which they had a right to expect on such an
occasion and in such a place. In whose name was this done?

[a] "Times" for Nov. 20, 1873.

Certainly not in the name of the Church, whose consent, had it been asked, would have been refused. Certainly not in the name of the State, whose law was infringed. Certainly not in the name of Christ, who was insulted in His religion. Certainly not in the name of God, who was insulted in His Son. In whose name, then, was it done? In the name of intellect—of intellect, as the French say, pure and simple, that would not be satisfied till every consideration, whether of law or religion, of conventionality or propriety, had been sacrificed to its demands, and creature-worship allowed admission into God's house—"Vis consili expers mole suâ ruit." Intellect has to be taught this lesson as well as brute force. It never shewed to less advantage or in worse taste than it did then. Imagine Hallam undertaking to lecture on constitutional law in the Hall of the Temple; or Kinglake offering his services at the Horse Guards to teach general officers how to handle their regiments; or Lord Selborne bidding the College of Surgeons listen to him on phlebotomy. But putting aside good breeding, as it was but a case of bearding the clergy, what was it that the justly distinguished Professor in coming forward intimated that they had yet to learn. He began by impressing upon them that truth required them to believe that there were eight religions; only whether there were just as many gods or not he would not explain. He finished by informing them that the two religions which presented most points of comparison, and whose fortunes were most similar, were one that had spread everywhere, and recognised but one God; and another that had spread nowhere, and recognised no God at all [b]—"Ne sutor ultra crepidam," even when that is philology. In most of the newspapers, however, this was paraded as a masterpiece, and passed for science.

Three weeks had not expired from its delivery before it was in turn eclipsed, and intellect-worshippers were chal-

[b] "Times" for Dec. 4, 1873.

lenged to assist at an entertainment every way more *spiri-tuel* and insinuating.

A certain Archbishop, who, by a singular coincidence, claims the cathedral as his own where this lecture was preached, is credited with having read a paper on "Cæsarism and Ultramontanism," before the members of an association called "Academia of the Catholic Religion," at his house in Westminster, on the evening of Dec. 23. It appeared at full length in next morning's "Times," in deference, probably, to the principles on which it went. It was a vindication, four columns of that paper long, of the absolute supremacy claimed for the Pope as head of the Church, on intellectual grounds, over the State; so intellectual indeed was it, as to be the perfection of logic, and in logical contradiction to Scripture, at the same time—"Let it be clearly understood," said the speaker, "that in these assertions I am vindicating to the Church her divine rights." Really! the speaker entertained no doubt, I presume, that the see of Rome was jointly founded by S. Peter and S. Paul, nor that Pius IX. represents them both. But had these Apostles been alive now, and acting in concert with deliberate purpose, they could not have met his English nominee more directly with a contradiction on every point, than they have by anticipation in their express teaching. They have not left him, literally, the shadow of a loop-hole between them. Each supplements, as if by design, what the other had left unsaid: "Let every soul be subject," says one, not excepting his own, therefore; "to every thing ordained by man," says the other; "I speak of supereminent powers in the abstract," says one; "I speak of a supereminent power in particular, called king or emperor, and his subordinates," says the other. If S. Peter preaches (ὑποτάσσεσθαι) subjection in general, this, S. Paul tells the Romans expressly, must be that of the soul, in other words, a living and active subjection, and to be rendered "for conscience sake." "Be subject to the powers that be," says he, writing to the uncircumcision, for "they are ordained by God." "Be subject to the king," says S. Peter, writing to the circumcision, "for the Lord's, that is, for Christ's sake.

Our Anglo-Roman prelate mistakes the postulates of intellect, premises and conclusion included, for Scriptural truth, and reveres them accordingly. If this is not intellect-worship, and if intellect-worship is not creature-worship, I know not what is. Ignorance may excuse the offender, but it will not whitewash the act; and creature-worship in sheep's clothing is infinitely more dangerous to society than the avowed wolf. Grandmammas are beguiled by a voice that affects child-like simplicity; and child-like dispositions are over-awed by a voice that addresses them gravely in the name of their grandmother.

Come to grief we must, if we allow ourselves to gravitate further in this direction. The reign of intellect is much too punishing to last long, or be popular with the million. It would hardly be installed, before there would be a "pronunciamento" got up against it in their name. It keeps society too much on the stretch; is always changing, always complaining, never at rest. When the Government that has just vacated was called "a harassing Government," everybody felt that no word could have described it better; everybody had become thoroughly sick of it on that account. But what was the secret of its composition? It was too intellectual by far. There were too many Professors concerned in it. If Prince Bismark really said on assuming the premiership of his country some years ago, "What I particularly want to do is to get rid of our Professors . . . to save Prussia from Professors," he never said a wiser thing. When Plato raved over the State that was administered by philosophers, it was not, it could not have been, the modern professor that he had in view. Plato would certainly never have trusted *him* with the framing of his education act. But the modern professor is altogether a new species. I remember "the time when he was not" myself. I assisted,

as the Ritualist would say, that is, I was present at his in-
carnation. He was just in his teens when the revolution
abroad proclaimed that men should grow beards; he embraced them with enthusiasm; he became conspicuous for
the length of his; he gauged intellect in others by the
length of theirs; he was inclined to cut everybody who had
none. It was his symbol of mind. The coming man, he
prophesied, would be of the Lombardic type. It escaped
him that long ears would have supplied a symbolism at once
more distinctive and appropriate—more distinctive, because
that distinction is already found *in rerum naturâ;* more
appropriate, because nature has placed them in closer prox-
imity to the brain.

I have no quarrel, personally, with the modern professor;
he is the best judge of his own happiness, if not of his own
consequence. But I rarely meet him without feeling that
he might be a happier man; and I never meet him without
feeling that society would be dissolved to-morrow, if it were
composed, or even governed, exclusively to-day of such as
he. Pure intellect is a disintegrating and disturbing, not
a consolidating or attracting force. It revels in contradic-
tions and condemnations. It knows its constructive powers
are few and limited: but that its capacities for pulling to
pieces are boundless. People talk of the want of charity
that prevails among religious sects. I never heard High or
Low Church speak of each other, under provocation, with half
the contempt which the modern professor evinces at all times
for his immediate fellows. I never pass an evening with
half-a-dozen of them, but I am set thinking of the battle of
the giants, waged by the frogs and mice.

Yet let it not be supposed for a moment that I consider
the modern professor as anything but a few steps in advance
of us all. He is at his worst nothing else but what all of us,
if we act on his assumption, must become. His assumption,
or rather the assumption of the system under which he has
been formed, is, that intellect makes the man. This is the

lie that *underlies* the principles which we have embraced in general as well as he. He is merely their embodiment or illustration. I say it is a lie; and I denounce it as such: first, because it is a lie whose palpable falsehood and deleterious influences I can verify without going outside myself; next, because I and mine are sufferers by it, whether we reject it or not; and hence, thirdly, because neither the State without the Church, nor the Church in league with the State, has any power to bind me to submit to that which is false in principle, and injurious to my best interest. It is false that intellect makes the man; because it is false that my intellect is myself, or anything but a subordinate part of myself either. I am certain that I am not it; nor is it my governor. If I cannot get it to do all I would, it shall at least obey me so far that it shall do nothing that I would not.

It was not from Scripture that I learnt this fact; though I am assured of it trebly from Scripture. With those who accept Scripture for their guide, I shall argue the point further on: at present I am only concerned to discuss it on principles which all must admit whose reason is sane.

Let me begin, then, by avowing that I have a great respect for my intellect; that I prize my intellect; that I am most thankful for the pains bestowed on it by others when I was young; and for the time which I have been able to bestow upon it since then myself. Yet, thanks to the education that was given in my day, I have not yet fallen into the error of estimating it too high. I know that it can create nothing, can invent nothing, can comprehend nothing that it was not meant to comprehend. It can comprehend nothing that is self-caused or infinite; nothing that is without beginning or end; nothing, probably, that transcends itself; as yet, it has failed even to discover whether the universe contains any finite natures which transcend its own; and if so, where, and under what conditions they live. As yet it cannot tell what the conditions of its own

existence would be, disjoined from the body. There may
be worlds into whose composition neither oxygen nor hy-
drogen, nitrogen nor carbon enter: myriads of beings, or
rather orders of beings, who would characterise the axioms
of Euclid and the laws of gravitation as so much infantine
prattle; the reasoning from premises to conclusion as un-
distinguishable from brute instinct. At present, how is
all information conveyed to the intellect, but through the
senses? For aught it can tell us to the contrary, it was
only meant to comprehend the visible things of the one
planet in which we live, and the revolutions of the others—
as distinct from their contents and component elements—
that it has ascertained, or thinks it has ascertained, to de-
pend on the same sun. At present, the objects of its con-
templation are limited as well as fixed; and the laws according to which it must act in all cases, beyond its control.
Even its own powers are not uniform; but are greater in
some than in others; and in all alike liable to be affected
by external influences. If it has instincts and energies of
its own, so has the body. My stomach abstracts nutriment
from what I eat and drink, just as my intellect abstracts
ideas from what I hear and see. If some have quicker intellects than ordinary, some have quicker digestions. I doubt
our intellects being acquainted with anything, as it is in
itself; or arriving at any conclusions otherwise than by
comparing one thing with another. What do we know of
straight lines in the abstract? What our intellect tells us
of them is that they are not crooked. Its powers, in short,
are not fitted to deal even with the things which exist
around us in *every way*, but in the definite way suitable
to our existing needs: on the same principle that beak and
talons are given to a hawk. If a hawk had not these,
he might perhaps live: but he would be unable to maintain himself as a hawk. If we had not those, neither
could we maintain ourselves as men. Even so, we must
have food provided for us on which our intellect can

feed; it cannot create food for itself; it cannot digest all food; in most cases it is, and it must be, taught how to feed, just as every chicken learns how to peck from the hen. Whatever may have been the course pursued in pre-historic times, it is clear that in every age whose records we have the means of consulting, man has, with a single exception, been brought into this world as a child, and commenced life as a learner. Before he can teach others, he must have been taught himself. Here we might commence speculating who taught his teacher? were speculation our line, which it is not. What Aristotle deliberately left unsolved in a formal treatise, need not be discussed in a tract. Besides, it would be necessary to enquire first, in each case, who *was* his teacher? I am content to interrogate my own intellect on the general question. If I said to it, "Think you, that had you been reared in a desert island, away from books, without teachers of any kind, without companions, without one of the social, moral, or intellectual influences of the nineteenth century to direct you, you would have been able to form the ideas of the nineteenth century for yourself?" it would answer, "Certainly not." If I continued, "Would you have been able to draw syllogisms, or form abstract ideas?" it would answer, "In all probability, neither the one nor the other." If I shifted my ground, and said, "Reared as you have been, do you remember ever originating an idea, that you could trace to no source but yourself?" it would reply, "Not to my knowledge. To the best of my belief every conception that I ever formed has been suggested to me from without, in some way or other, though now and then its sources have been so completely lost sight of, that I may have been for a time tempted to consider it an original thought. Afterwards, something occurred to shew me when and how it arose. Sometimes it was a mere corollary to some position imbibed from my teachers; sometimes a mere application of universals to particulars; sometimes it was suggested by a kindred idea, which another had dropped; sometimes conveyed through books, sometimes through speech; sometimes it was suggested by the action of bird, beast, or fish; sometimes by changes in inanimate nature." My own intellectual powers are but ordinary; still, arguing from such experience as I have gained from them, I can maintain unhesitatingly that, in practice, the intellect gets all its information from hints, from hints supplied to it in nine cases out of ten from without, and that men are called original thinkers from the activity and dexterity with which they make use of such hints—not because the intellect which is only rubbed against itself can ever produce sparks. In my school-days, when we had subjects given us for verses or themes, hints were read out to us ordinarily by the head-master, which we either copied down or carried away in our minds. And the best verses and themes were certainly done by those who remembered most hints. Even in mature years, I imagine, most men who contemplate making a book on any subject, begin by reading up all that they can possibly find written on it by others—whether they have the honesty to confess this afterwards or not, shewing how every body shrinks instinctively from thinking out a subject for himself. If we turn to the annals of Science we see that it advances, in general, step by step: or that the door has been opened to its mightiest outbursts by some unforeseen incident in which it had no hand. The story told of Newton and the apple is not peculiar to the apple or to Newton either; it merely symbolises a general rule. For how many centuries had men been cutting their names on trees, or taking impressions from seals, before it occurred to them to print books. For how many centuries had painting and architecture been travailling with children, before children were born to them like Raphael and Michael Angelo? The trade winds, not science, piloted Columbus to the far west. The laziness of a boy, not science, made the steam-engine self-acting. An act of parliament for the preservation of woods discovered the secret of smelting iron with coal; a chance slip in the laboratory the secret of extracting silver from lead. The enlightenment in which we live, and which we are too frequently tempted to look upon as our own offspring, represents the accumulated achievements of the human intellect, after efforts abortive, and failures innumerable, in all former ages, to which we have merely contributed our quota; and this quota, subtracted from the sum total preceding it, would be found to be small indeed, or rather it would crumble away in our hands. For it stands to reason that the collective intellect of no single age, deprived of the experiences of all former ages, could succeed in producing anything like what we call civilization, any more than any single intellect that had never been sharpened by contact with other intellects, anything like what we call science. If fire were to sweep away all our libraries and works of art to-day, and war or pestilence all our men of science to-morrow, our children, we may be sure, would evolve tails instead of heads the day after; and in another century might either be learning to use chopsticks from the Chinese, or quietly settling down into jelly-fish.

Accordingly, we must beware of over-rating what our intellect can do for us, or was meant to do for us, even in this life, taking things as they are, and putting the supernatural on one side. Its work lies in a much smaller compass than we are apt to think. Its energies are limited to the objects of sense, and it apprehends them but relatively to our uses and needs; its knowledge results from discoveries, and the superstructure which it builds on them. But, in nine cases out of ten, its discoveries are not original, but suggested to it by hints from others; and the conclusions which it draws from them are far oftener false than true. Half-an-hour's conversation with any beings who were present when this earth was made, and could explain to us the secrets of its composition in familiar language, would enlighten us on more points than all the savans of the nineteenth century could discover for us in their lives.

I have not done testifying against my intellect that it is not myself, nor the best part of myself either. "Mens cujusque, is est quisque," said the ghost of Scipio. I have not forgotten the transport of enthusiasm which these words kindled in me, when I first read them. And I then translated *mens*, "understanding," with Scheller and Facciolati. Afterwards I saw, 1. That *mens* was to be taken in a wider and more generic sense, and comprehended other things besides intellect; and 2. That the ghost put forward a two-fold claim; a claim of immortality for mind in general, and a claim of individuality for every mind in particular. I felt a greater admiration for the ghost, after unravelling his meaning, than I had before. To have uttered those four words was more to his honour really, than to have vanquished Hannibal : though they afford no countenance to the favourite maxim of the nineteenth century. When the ghost taught, "My mind is myself," he disclosed a profound truth; when the nineteenth century says, "My intellect is myself," it lies.

There was another epigrammatic utterance which caused me much enthusiasm when I first heard of it; though, in many respects, it does so no longer. It is the celebrated enthymeme of Descartes: "Cogito, ergo sum." I am still grateful to it for the reaction it produced from materialism, but its logic has been over-rated. "Comedo, ergo sum," would have been just as convincing; and a cow might argue just as forcibly from this, as a savant. Besides, where was the gain of proving what required no proof, being obvious to the senses? But had Descartes been desirous of establishing any distinctive conclusion about man, he should have advanced a step further, and said boldly, *Conscius sum, ergo resurgam :* "I have a conscience, therefore I shall rise again." My conscience dictates this conclusion, "proprio motu." My intellect merely puts it into logical form, and then subscribe to it *I must*. Neither my conscience, nor my intellect, is myself; but both my intellect and I bow to my conscience. It is our master. Though not my whole self, it is my better self: every part of me quakes, when it is disobeyed; my whole man is at rest *only*, when this part of me reigns supreme.

I shrink instinctively from bodily pain, and am always ready to run away from it when I can, and to shorten or diminish it when compelled to submit to it; but when it is over, I can not only look back to it in most cases without a shudder, but at times with infinite pleasure. As for bodily weaknesses and ailments, I bear with them while they last, and invite sympathy for them from others. If they have not been caused by my own sin or folly, I have no scruple in owning them, and pleading them every now and then to excuse my shortcomings. Again, it happens frequently that I am vexed with my intellect for not understanding things that I would give worlds to learn, or for forgetting things I would give worlds to remember. Still, in my cooler moments, neither my want of memory, nor my want of intelligence, depresses my spirits in any perceptible degree. I can be merry over both. I cannot, if I wished it, look upon either as a visitation, much less a crime. I try to compensate for the defects of the one by keeping a common-place book, of the other by attending popular lectures; and in this way I jog on cheerfully enough, in spite of both.

It is another thing altogether when either my bodily ailments have been caused by any misdeeds of mine, or when my ignorance or forgetfulness proceeds from neglect or wilfulness; in that case another actor appears quickly on the scene, who claims to speak with authority; and the whole character of the action is changed. What was in itself a mere forget, suffering, or misadventure, is certain to fill me with shame and remorse from henceforth, in spite of myself. *In spite of myself,* I say; for it is literally so, then, with a vengeance. At such times I feel as if I were literally two persons. On one side there is myself struggling vigorously to get rid of the load that weighs me down; apologising for my flesh, if it is my flesh that has committed the wrong; or for my intellect, if it is against my intellect that the charge lies. On the other side there is a power standing over me, which I feel to be part of myself, though it prevents my rising. By way of eluding its grasp, I try to inspire my intellect with a nonchalance that I would fain were mine. I bid it divert itself with new topics; I forbid its going back to the past in thought; I bid it erase from memory what distresses us both; I patch up my exterior as best I can; I put on a settled look and unruffled air, meeting my friends as though I had nothing upon my mind, had done nothing I should be ashamed they should know. All in vain; there is the vulture gnawing at my vitals, of which an old myth speaks. I dread each moment that I am left alone. I cannot help subscribing to the verdict that has been passed on my conduct by the voice within me, though I would dissent from it if I could. It warned me beforehand, and I disobeyed it, therefore it was not myself who spoke. I disobeyed it, and it is making me wretched against my will; I am doubly convinced, therefore, that it is not myself now; yet it both was and is within me still; nobody knows of its existence besides myself. And whether I can say what it is or not; and although I can say that it is neither my body, my intellect, nor myself; still I am equally certain that it belongs to me, and is, or should be, arbiter of all I do. Though I had learnt and mastered every science under the sun, I could never know what it was to be happy for one moment, as long as that voice told me that I was doing wrong. And certainly there is no pleasure that I ever derive from intellectual acquirements, or bodily luxuries of any kind, to compare with the charm of an unruffled and unclouded conscience,—a charm which cannot be bought for gold.

I am unable to describe this, indeed, half so well as I must always feel it; and may be, most people would say the same. Possibly this may arise from our not knowing as much of our conscience as we ought; I never read any thing on conscience that satisfied me yet, and when I turn my thoughts inwards on it, I find its introspection of all tasks the most difficult and delicate, arising probably from its being my superior. Of course the Schoolmen said next to nothing about it in their theological Sums, because, though named frequently by S. Paul, it was barely noticed by Aristotle. Of course Roman Catholic divines have never approached it but with fear and trembling, because the modern assertion of the rights of conscience has robbed them of, at least, three-fourths of their sway. And of course, lastly, the political jargon of liberty of conscience, about which so much is said on the hustings, and the ideal jargon about inner consciousness, imported in such profusion from Germany, must tend alike to lower its credit and impair its lustre in the eyes of men, till it has been regularly disengaged from both. Even Bishop Sanderson in his admirable treatise, than which I thought I never had read a better thirty years ago, from having been trained in "the Schools," mis-defines it "a habit of the practical intellect;" I might equally well affirm this of my sense of taste. I never see honey or anchovies on the table, but it petitions for them—and why? Because on all former occasions it has found them good. Its appeal is strictly syllogistic : "Honey is to my liking. This is honey; *Ergo*, let me have some." For all that, would anybody tolerate his sense of taste being defined a habit of his practical intellect? Conscience is as superior to the intellect as the intellect is to the senses. And surely a king may walk on two legs without being taken either for a professor or a pigeon. People were given, in former days, to argue rather from names than from things; accordingly, they thought it a proof that conscience belonged to the intellect, because it was named from *science.* Bishop Butler, in his golden essay upon "the nature of Virtue," shook himself free from this conceit, though even he shrank from determining what conscience was. After all, the name which it now bears was current in Greek as well as in Latin before the New Testament was written, and therefore must have been invented before the Gospel was preached. It is used in the New Testament, moreover, in more senses than one; consequently the soundest argument that could have been drawn from its name was, that the thing signified by it had been recognised in heathen times, and among the Gentiles more notably than the Jews; for in the Old Testament it has no special name of its own, being expressed by two words, one properly meaning "spirit," and the other "heart." But the fact is, we might as well set about proving that people are born with noses, as that they are born with consciences. Where there are no looking-glasses people rarely see their nose; but looking-glasses are not needed to shew people their conscience. The sole difficulty consists in determining what it is. If, however, it is the same in all persons, anybody may without presumption state the conclusions at which he has arrived respecting his own. Careful reflection, then, has convinced me that it is a sentiment or faculty distinct from the intellect, distinct from the affections, distinct from the senses, distinct from the will itself. It evinces a settled indifference to the subjects on which the intellect is employed; it awards no praise to the intellect for superior acuteness, or for its grandest discoveries, viewed in themselves; it rebukes the intellect for any neglect of duty just as peremptorily, and with just as much freedom, as it rebukes the senses. To its mere shortcomings and infirmities it is lenient enough. The peasant is not rebuked by his conscience for not being a mathematician; nor the mathematician, should he get incapacitated for work as he grows old.

Conscience never stoops to notice, regret, or resent any mistakes into which the intellect may chance to fall within the limits of its own province. It is averse to falsehood of any sort, of course; but error in speculation is *not* falsehood, till it is cherished after it has been proved false. Besides, nature avenges every perversion or misapprehension of her laws so promptly, that people rarely persist in maintaining any such errors with their eyes open. Even if they do, conscience leaves them in general to learn wisdom by experience. For aught it cares, anybody may still hold that the sun goes round the earth, instead of the earth going round the sun. It harbours no resentment against those who formerly taught the first; and passes no encomium on those who pride themselves on having learnt the last. But if ever the intellect should happen to cross the frontier, and meddle with questions relating to morals and conduct, conscience is in a ferment at once, and stings like a bee. Woe to the intellect if it should reason amiss, or start from false principles, on these points. Ignorance will not avail even to palliate its backslidings. Conscience armed Socrates against the sophists, and brought him in victor almost without striking a blow. Their logical subtleties were demolished at each swoop of his broad-sword. Conscience armed Luther against the schoolmen; they were welcome to any conclusions they pleased on speculative dogma. Their false casuistry sealed their fate, and that of the cause they upheld. Europe was of one mind in breaking with them, even if it was not of one mind in accepting Luther.

The subjects, obviously, which interest the conscience most are those which occupy the senses and the affections. It is on these that its attention is most concentrated, and in reference to these that its cautions are loudest, and its decisions most authoritative for praise or blame. It evidently considers all that tends to form or develope the character

its special province. But beyond comparison, it testifies
to there being more evil than good in us; and hence its
praises for doing right are fainter and less persistent than
its rebukes for doing wrong.

With the will, which more than anything else constitutes
the man, it is for the same reason almost always in con-
flict, often disobeyed, though never disobeyed with im-
punity, to the last claiming to be heard, except, indeed,
it has been drugged. For by the combined action of all
four—intellect, affections, senses, and will—it will happen
occasionally, that conscience may be stupified for a time,
and life brought to a sudden close before it can awake.

From all which it follows incontestably that conscience
was given us for a very special purpose of its own, distinct
from, and vastly superior to, that served by the intellect.
Intellect was given us to explore, analyse, and turn to our
present use the world surrounding us: conscience was given
us to form the man. Knowledge was to be the achievement
of the one, character the other. "Nihil esse in intellectu,
quod non prius fuerit in sensu," is a doctrine that I can
accept willingly for my intellect; but it must be just reversed for my conscience; conscience is not indebted in
any way for its ideas of right and wrong to the senses.
It was impressed with those ideas when it was born; it is
inseparable from them, it measures every thing coming
under its cognisance by their standard, now. It enlarges
or modifies them by intercourse, not with *natura naturata*
—the world surrounding us—but with other consciences.
Yet that they were the invention of other consciences any
more than its own, it cannot pretend for a moment; nor
could any rational account be given of their hold over it
if they were. The intellect might as well be credited with
having originated the laws of motion or gravitation which
it has discovered in nature; as conscience, the standard of
right and wrong, which it finds in its own depths. But if
conscience neither invented this standard, nor acquired it

through the senses, how came we by it? Well, unless conscience can also decide this question for us, it is obvious that we have nothing else within us that can. Yet the very naming of this standard fills the conscience with awe. Conscience warns us against supposing that it is self-sown; conscience whispers to us tremblingly that it proceeds from a higher power, and from a source unseen. Conscience cannot pretend but that it owes infinitely more obedience to this standard, than it can claim from us. Conscience must further own that it has no claim to obedience but what it derives from this standard; that it never departs from this standard, but it is self-condemned, and feels its authority gone. Conscience will, if searchingly cross-questioned, tell us in addition, that there is nothing it loves half so well as this standard; that there is nothing for which it yearns half so much as to have this standard more perfectly revealed to it, and to be able to guarantee its better observance proportionably by the whole man. Conscience is just as little satisfied with its own present ideas of it as with its own achievements in connexion with it. Nothing would fill conscience with more rapture than to see an improvement in both. Conscience groans unutterably for a revelation of ideal justice and mercy, together with truth and love, and a succession of characters formed on them in their perfection. Conscience feels morally certain that both must exist in their full beauty somewhere, and that even the imperfect characters which it forms here are destined for somewhere else. Conscience cannot divest itself of its presentiment, of its inmost conviction—call it by what name you will—that the grave which closes over this life only discloses another.

Particular consciences of course differ in their perception and estimate of these things. I will only say that I never yet probed *one* that was not alive to them; and invariably, where they encountered a cold response, there were obvious reasons for wishing that there was no such thing as conscience at all. Lucretius admitted, while he deplored the fact. Born genius as he was, the world is farther than ever from his views. A new religion, by staking its credentials upon the very doctrine which he strove to eradicate, and then gaining and maintaining a hold upon society throughout the world, such as no religion has ever done before or since, has proved to demonstration on which side the instincts of mankind are ranged. And never were they expressed in finer or more cosmopolitan language, than they have been by two master-minds in our own vernacular; one speaking for nature, and the other for culture :—

> "To be, or not to be, that is the question:
> . . . . To die—to sleep—
> No more; and, by a sleep, to say we end
> The heart-ache, and the thousand natural shocks
> That flesh is heir to—'tis a consummation
> Devoutly to be wished; to die, to sleep—
> To sleep ! perchance to dream ; aye, there's the rub ;
> For in that sleep of death what dreams may come,
> When we have shuffled off this mortal coil,
> Must give us pause . . . . for . . . . who would fardels bear,
> To grunt and sweat under a weary life ;
> But that the dread of something after death—
> The undiscovered country, from whose bourn
> No traveller returns—puzzles the will ;
> And makes us rather bear the ills we have,
> Than fly to others that we know not of.
> Thus conscience does make cowards of us all !"

Translate this into every known language; interpret it to anybody possessed of the heart of a man, and it will send a thrill through him. Again, what educated person, except when his fears overpowered him, could be found dissenting from this :—

> "And that must end us; that must be our cure,
> To be no more ? sad cure ! for who would lose,
> Though full of pain, this intellectual being—
> Those thoughts that wander through eternity—

To perish rather ? swallow'd up and lost
In the wide womb of uncreated night,
Devoid of sense and motion."

Everybody recoils instinctively from annihilation; nobody loves wrong-doing for its own sake; everybody would
rather be good than bad. *If all consciences had only fair
play, there would be no such thing as crime.* But to have
fair play, they must be educated, and not left to themselves. There is no part of us, left to itself, that will not
become foul. Conscience, like everything else that is in
man—like man himself—must be developed by culture;
and culture requires that its inherent powers should be
called into play by congenial exercise; and its infirmities,
together with the artificial impediments to its unshackled
action which abound in us, checked or exterminated. "Conscius sum, ergo resurgam." Our instinct of immortality is
the correlative to our instinct of right and wrong; and it
is by these, beyond any question, our noblest instincts,
much more than the discursive faculty which we call reason, that we are distinguished from brutes, and should regulate our lives as men. Put your hand on your heart, O
man, wherever you have been born—whatever language
you speak—and confess honestly, that no intellectual success you ever achieved could indemnify you for the loss of
a " mens conscia recti;" no intellectual failure that you can
remember, ever afflicted you with the remorse inseparable
from the consciousness of having done wrong.

They who would regenerate society, or elevate man, are
bound to bestow most pains in developing his grandest instincts. In the educationary programme, which, after fight-
ing over till we lost our heads, we have made national, we
have committed a three-fold sin. We have sinned against
every principle of common sense in making education begin
and end with the intellect; we have sinned against our
Maker in proclaiming that we have nothing in us superior

to the intellect to educate; we have sinned against mankind, let alone ourselves, in proclaiming that it is to the cultivation of the intellect alone that we must look for the redress of every social plague, and commit all our hopes of securing the peace, the well-being, and final humanizing of the world. Since England became a nation till now, history cannot tell of any general scheme for educating her people more socially destructive, more philosophically false, than this. It might have been concerted in pandemonium, for the effects that are certain to ensue from it, if it is allowed full play; seeing that it has a direct tendency to disintegrate society link by link, and end by setting every man against his neighbour. That which evokes the affections, forms the character, raises the man, reminds him of his responsibilities, informs him of his dependence on a higher Power, discourses to him of rewards and punishments in a world to come, presses on him his duty to his fellow-men, which is the foundation of all law and order, and keeps passion in check with a rod more terrible than that of the civil judge—this he is invited to put on one side, and therefore dissuaded from taking any pains to improve. And that which begets pride, and inspires no love, creates no social bond, exerts no check upon conduct, keeps the attention fixed on the things of this world exclusively, knows nothing, and affects to care for nothing beyond them; ministers to jealousy, disputings, and estrangement, between man and man; on this he is ordered to spare no pains in cultivating, under the expectation that when cultivated, it is to afford him a panacea for all his woes.

Thus the knowledge which two thousand years ago was pronounced heaven-born—"*E cælo descendit, γνῶθι σεαυτόν*" —we are teaching our children to consign to the shelf. And the motto which was devised for England on the eve of her proudest triumph—"England expects every man to do his duty"—we have degraded into, "England expects every man to learn his three r's." But he was a greater philosopher, and a profounder statesman, who bequeathed this motto to us, than they whose names were inscribed on the back of the Public Education Act of 1870 ; and I have no fear which will live longest in the minds of men, or in the annals of this country. But I think the day may come when posterity may be more puzzled over this paradox, even than we are now : how one who must have passed a brilliant examination in the politics of Aristotle and Plato when he was young, and could have dilated in sheet upon sheet on the prominence given to moral training in both ; who but the other day groaned over the apathy with which Bishop Butler is now regarded by his contemporaries, should have been the prime mover and legislator of a system of general education, in which there is absolutely no provision made for educating anything besides the intellect : absolutely no principle laid down, even in passing, from which it might be gathered that man has anything in him besides intellect which is worth a thought. I have studiously refrained from saying a word about religion in this chapter, as I wished to avoid introducing any matter which might prevent the primary question from being argued on its own merits. Accordingly, putting the supernatural altogether on one side, I denounce the Public Education Act of 1870 as being treason to humanity. In times like these, when liberty of conscience supplies every political following with so much cant, is it not unpardonable that any statesman should need reminding that man *has* a conscience ?

CHAPTER II.

"RESURGAM" is the key-stone of the arch on which Christianity reposes; but that arch is the human heart itself. When Bishop Butler said of Christianity that it was a republication of natural religion, he disclosed the secret of its success and hold upon man. It offered nothing that was attractive, and a good deal that was unpalatable, to his lower nature. It all but ignored, except when it disparaged, his intellect. It went straight to the seat of authority. It addressed itself to a power within man, whose sovereignty was unquestioned, in offering consciences at once the information and the assistance for which they had hitherto pined in vain. It came to them with a message of love direct from their Superior. It identified Him, the Creator of all things, with the source from which their ideas of right and wrong were derived. It explained the secret of their hopes and fears by unfolding to them the tribunal at which they would have to render account, when this life was past. Above all, it set before them, for present purposes, a perfect Exemplar; offering them, in the same breath, a code of instructions, and superhuman assistance for taking His mould. By these means, conjointly, it undertook, in preparing man for heaven, to minister to his improvement on earth: to assist consciences in forming higher and more perfect characters than any they had ever achieved as yet, and raise man to a level he had never attained before.

This is what the religion of Christ professed at the outset, in challenging competition with all other religions; and this is the explanation of its having been almost immediately taken into partnership by the civil power, after sufficient time had been given for proving that it could be as good as its promise. The Roman empire became Christian, I say, only when it had been proved by sufficient experience that Christianity manufactured better men and better citizens than all the other religions put together that had preceded it. On this account it was, that from having been at first proscribed, and then tolerated, it rose by common consent to be the only religion allowed in the civilised world.

It would be this still, but for the damnable Inquisitions and Holy Wars—I denounce them in the strongest terms allowed by our formularies—that, by claiming its sanction, have sapped its credit. It is the recoil from their accursed principles which has made the nations of Europe regard with distrust the faith that civilised them, and mis-invoke liberty of conscience, to aid men in casting off a religion distinguished from all other religions, in having been designed primarily *to aid the conscience.* Luckily, there is a text-book that has survived these corruptions, pure and unadulterated, to which Christianity can appeal in proof of her original aim and principles; and that text-book still retains its hold upon the public mind. For it is not the Bible, really, that has ever suffered from the criticisms so freely lavished on it, but only the interpretations put upon it by man. Its worst foes are those glosses which pervert its sense.

It is to this text-book that I shall go for what I am about to say, and to this text-book alone; for it is absolutely nothing more than its true meaning that I am solicitous about. It is the one arbiter whose rulings Christians of every denomination are bound to uphold; and so long as the legislation of a country is based upon it, or not at variance with it, neither they nor I can have any right to complain. But we have the strongest right to demand that neither the richest nor the poorest among us shall be compelled by law to contribute or to conform to any departure from its indisputable principles in bringing up our children, and I therefore call upon Christians of all denominations to join in declaring that this is a question in which fathers and mothers of families are most concerned, and which it would be the height of injustice to insist on being decided for them irrevocably by professors or by statesmen either.

When I stated that Christianity professed to prepare man for heaven, and in doing so to better his condition upon earth : and also that the Bible was its text-book : I stated, in effect, that it had something to say on the education of man as well for the present as for the world to come, and that it had said this in the Bible.

What, accordingly, does the Bible say, and on which culture does it lay most stress, that of the head or the heart? On this point, I make bold to say, there cannot seriously be two opinions. Cicero says the ancient world was divided as to whether the seat of the mind was in the heart or the brain. There can be no question but that in the Old and New Testament, with one consent, almost exclusive reference is made to the heart. By the heart, indeed, a Jew would often mean the conscience ; as I pointed out some pages back. "Good and evil proceed from the heart," says our Lord ; and the character depends on which of them abounds there most : "For out of the abundance of the heart the mouth speaketh." "That which cometh out of a man," He said on another occasion, "that it is which defiles the man." Then, in the next breath, lest His meaning should be misapprehended, He adds : "For from within, out of the heart of men"—not the head—"proceed evil thoughts," &c. According to the teaching of the Old Testament, the wickedness of man which caused the deluge, consisted in this, that "every imagination of the thoughts of his heart" was habitually bent on evil. "The heart is deceitful above all things and desperately wicked," says one prophecy : "All the house of Israel are uncircumcised in the heart," says another. Whenever the reformation of man is in question, he is to be healed through the heart ; "My Son, give me thine heart," says the Preacher. "A new heart also will I give you, and a new spirit will I put within you: and I will take away the stony heart out of your flesh, and I will give you an heart of flesh," says the Prophet. "Thou shalt love the Lord thy God with all thy heart, . . . and with all thy mind," said our Lord, putting the heart foremost, and mind in the background. When the first Gentile was evangelised, he asked, "What doth hinder me to be baptised?" and the reply was : "If thou believest with all thine heart, thou mayest." For, as the Apostle of the Gentiles afterwards expressed it, "With the heart man believeth unto righteousness," not the head. This, again, we learn from him was where God worked also. "God hath sent the Spirit of His Son into your hearts," not your heads. And again : "That Christ may dwell in your hearts by faith." And again : "The peace of God, which passeth all understanding, shall keep your hearts and thoughts," where hearts are placed first. Our Lord says finally : "Blessed are the pure in heart, for they shall see God:" not "blessed are they who have clear heads."

The prominence given to the heart in these passages, and scores more that they cannot fail to suggest, is enhanced immensely when we come to contrast it with the slender and unfrequent allusions ever. made to the head. The Greek word λόγος occurs again and again in the New Testament, but never in the sense of "the reason;" the Greek words for intellect, understanding, and their cognates, occur surprisingly seldom, and not, in any case that I can recal, to do honour to the faculties they represent. Thoughts are, perhaps, oftener ascribed to the heart than not ; and in one place we have this expression : "lest they should understand with their hearts." Once, and but once, the understanding is named in the Gospels, and then the action of our Lord upon it is deeply significant : "Then opened He their *understanding* (νοῦν) that they might understand the Scriptures." Till then its utmost efforts

had failed in unravelling their true meaning. Agreeably
with this, S. Paul congratulates the Ephesians who be-
lieved "that the eyes of their understanding had been
enlightened." Elsewhere, the Jews and Gentiles, who
rejected the Gospel, are successively described by him as
having their "intellects blinded."

In all these passages the drift of Scripture is as clear as
can be, and in harmony with itself all through. The heart
is everywhere regarded as determining the character of
every man for good or for ill, and as being diseased—diseased, because torn by the conflicting principles of right and
wrong, and at war with the conscience. Scripture meddles
but in this strife. All its commands, menaces, and ob-
jurgations; all its appeals, exhortations, and remedies—human or superhuman—are thus addressed to the heart; not,
indeed, that man is addressed in them as if he were nothing
but heart. When it speaks of evil thoughts coming from
the heart, its meaning is not that he thinks with his heart,
but that his thoughts are good or evil according to the tone
of his heart. The origin of their moral quality, not their
abstract origin, is the thing in question. It sits as censor
upon thoughts and words only so far as they affect practice:
on conduct in general as distinct from other acts; it has
nothing to say to language, reasoning, or knowledge, considered in themselves and apart from this; it is far from
putting either slur or constraint upon them in their own
special province; its reference to the intellect and to the
reason is exceptional, and in general without significance.
But there are passages, as I have shewn already, where we
find the intellect and the reason both told plainly that there
are subjects which are beyond them in their present state,
without light from above. "The natural man," says the
Apostle, "receiveth not the things of the Spirit of God;
for they are foolishness unto him : *neither can he know them,*
because they are spiritually discerned." In other words,
what Scripture says to the intellect and to the reason in

more places than one amounts to this: "If you attempt
to read me just as any other book,. I tell you beforehand, my meaning will escape you both." Yet this is
only said by the way and to prevent mistakes. It bids
man everywhere listen to it with his heart. "Only
give me your heart," it says to him, "and you may do
what you will with your head, and with your body too.
So long as your thoughts are not evil, you may think on
what subjects you will; make any discoveries you can in
the outer world that will tend to your comfort or amuse-
ment; develope your bodily powers to any extent of which
they are capable—"Adultery, fornication, uncleanness, lasci-
viousness, idolatry, witchcraft, hatred, variance, emulations,
wrath, strife, seditions, heresies, envyings, murders, drunken-
ness, revellings," such are the social demons against which
I declare war to the knife; from all such debasing and de-
filing pests, if all who profess me, will only conform to my
precepts, I engage to disinfect one nation after another.
But again: "The fruit of the Spirit is love, joy, and peace"—
not history, nor geography, nor mathematics, nor chemistry,
nor geology, nor athletics. God does not bid you learn
geography; neither, therefore, will He help you to learn
geography; except, indeed, when you learn it, or anything
else, as being your duty, and then He will. All that God
specially bids you do, He will help you to do; and your
moral duties belong to this class. But, intellectually, you
may employ your time as you will; He leaves you free.
Moreover, you will search in vain for information in His
revealed word on any point which your natural faculties
ought to discover for themselves. For all natural objects,
and for all phenomena connected with them—for making
observations on them, and drawing conclusions from them—
He refers you to the hand and eye; to the reason and intellect, which are common possessions of all men; to the
tastes and talents which are the special possession of some,
to supply you with all the knowledge man was formed

D

for acquiring in his present state, and to which every man was likewise formed for contributing.

By all means choose your profession and calling in life. Pursue those studies by all means in which you think you can excel most. You will be examined by Him hereafter in the things which you have *done, not* in the things which you have *learnt* here. Learned, or unlearned, you will be sure of a place in His kingdom, if you have done well. The cup of cold water given in the name of a disciple will benefit you more *there*, than high classical or mathematical honors. Still you will find nothing in the Bible to forbid your making this world more habitable, or yourself more civilized. Every faculty that you have, was given you to be cultivated; and the higher the perfection you can achieve for it the better. Only learn to behave well before all things, even in this life. You must live for others, as well as for yourself, whether you wish it or not; and knowledge without good conduct will neither conduce to their well-being, nor your own. When you regulate your life by your conscience, and your conscience by God's law, my task is done. In everything else, consult your own tastes, and be free.

Such, in familiar language, is the system of education which the Bible prescribes for man; and I certainly know of no philosophy that ever devised a truer, or one more calculated to raise man individually to the highest perfection attainable by him in this life, let alone fitting him for the next. It is a system of education suitable for man all the world over, and for all classes and ages equally, laying down the same law for all; intent on engaging everybody to behave his best, in whatever circumstances he may have been born and bred; to whatsoever studies or employments he may have been led by his own tastes. It proceeds on the assumption, which no sane person would think of disputing, that the faculty which needs most uniform cultivation in all, as determining their character—as determining their influence upon society for good—is not the intellect, but the conscience; that if their conscience can only be got to act as it should, neither their intellect nor their passions will ever lead them astray; but their whole man will be set on promoting their own happiness and that of their neighbour from the highest of motives, and with settled purpose. It proceeds on the assumption, that what society needs most, is a specific against disorder—the disorder that springs from crime. Accordingly, it concentrates all its efforts on strengthening those moral forces within man, which, if every man heeded as he ought, crime would be nowhere, though every law in our criminal code were repealed.

Contrast this with the wretched assumption of our Elementary Education Act of 1870, designed to provide for the entire moulding of children of both sexes from five years old to thirteen. It as good as tells them they have nothing in them worth educating but their intellect; that all the education they need have, is comprised in the subjects on which they are examined in school; and that they will be fit for making their way in life when it is over. In a few of the books which are put into their hands to teach them to read, there may chance to be some moral lessons scattered up and down; but of morality, as a theme to be learnt and practised, they never hear, and of conscience they are left to form their own ideas, as best they may. For they never need hear a prayer said unless they like, even where prayers are said; even when religion is taught, they are free not to learn. Or let them affectionate both ever so, they may have their tender aspirations rudely shaken out of them: for their local authorities may summarily deprive them of both, without consulting them, by a stroke of the pen. Ignorance, they may come to think some day, is the only sin anybody can commit. Formerly they burnt for heresy, as though it were the worst of crimes; now they have made non-attendance at the board-school punishable with fine or imprisonment, as though ignorance was the next worst. Ludicrous, if it were not likewise monstrous, paradox, to see the modern professor and the mediæval inquisitor shaking hands across the bridge of time, and saying, "Well! we are agreed so far, that, as long as intellect is properly looked after, morality may be left out in the cold."

To complete the picture, we have merely to suppose the State thus accosted some twenty or thirty years hence by one of the clever unscrupulous intellects it has thus educated: "What business have you to punish me for thieving or murdering? I was never taught these things were wrong. I never heard a word against them in your board-schools all the years I attended them. Father never cared about my learning anything there that I was not examined in; and there was no examination in anything of this kind. Why should not people be allowed to steal from each other if they please? it is as fair for one as the other; and those who have got too much ought not to be protected by law against those that are starving. Then, as to murdering; why should not people be left to take care of themselves? If I kill Thomas, what are Thomas' friends about, not to be down upon me? why should they or the country be put to the cost of getting Jack the hangman to do their work? Why cannot we fight out our own quarrels without a policeman? Who was it that *told you* stealing and murder were wrong? [I say you have been grossly imposed upon. One was voted a crime by the weak, the other by the rich; but I am just as much entitled to be heard on these points as they, and I denounce them as specimens of class-legislation of the worst kind. I have certainly heard talk of a God and of the Ten Commandments out of school now and then: but it seems incredible you can make more account of either than I do, or you would have seen to my learning somewhat about both when I was young."

Some of us may affect indifference to what may be the condition of the State twenty or thirty years hence, but the fact is, we are all of us parties to what the State now is: all, therefore, responsible for whatever it may become. In the same way, we are all of us parties to the Elementary Education Act of 1870, as long as it remains law; and it would be pitiful indeed if, because it concerned the children of the poor more immediately than our own, we shut our eyes just where they could not be opened too wide. We that are Christians cannot dispense ourselves from the obligation of examining it on Christian principles; of enquiring whether it can ever be safe or suitable for Christian children; whether it is calculated to leave them better or worse Christians than they were before. Judged by this test, its essential features proclaim themselves.

How any men, calling themselves Christians, can have been talked into the idea that a system of education for young children, from five years old and upwards—in which the subject of morals is left out, and religious observances and religious instruction are publicly declared optional; in which the intellect is treated throughout as being the only thing in a child worth developing, and secular learning the only provision made for acquainting him with his duties to God, his neighbour, and himself in after life—could be accepted, I won't say without contradicting, but without insulting Scripture, it is for them to explain. My own matured opinion of it, confirmed by experience, is, that it might have been framed in accordance with instructions from the apostate Julian; and putting every notion of a Church out of sight, and looking only to the Bible for my warrant, I maintain that to submit to it permanently would be to betray Christianity.

CHAPTER III.

THE Elementary Education Act of 1870 may be characterised as a party sop at its introduction, and an incentive to national suicide in its *dénouement*. It was one of those measures adventured obviously to keep the Liberal party together, and to curry favour for them with the country. Nobody would think of charging either even of the two statesmen, in whose names it went forth, with having originated or wished for it as it now stands. And had their more potent chief resolutely set his back against the wall, and said, "I will have none of it," it would never have become law. Unfortunately, the composition of his Cabinet was such that intellect outweighed character. It contained administrators that inspired the very reverse of confidence. It numbered too many professors in it by half for its principles. There was the parsimonious and flippant, not over scrupulous, but eminently astute, Chancellor of the Exchequer to begin with. It needed not his sagacity to foresee that if the annual grant for education went on increasing till it reached the amount actually required, it must figure before long as a formidable charge in the Budget, extinguishing his schemes for a surplus year by year. And how was it possible to pass for a successful Chancellor of the Exchequer without a surplus? Further, as long as it was supplied from the public purse of the nation, it was sure to be lavishly expended; and just one of those charges which, from the interest now taken in education, everybody would be ready to condemn a minister for attempting to control or economise. The history of the revised Code proved this.

I dare say he never slept as guardian of the public purse more soundly than on the night it was decided that this charge should be transferred to the local rates. Nor should I be surprised if, as he retired to rest, he muttered something to himself about having killed two birds with one stone. However, had the other bird survived, it would never have disturbed his own rest after this; but then he had a colleague, a great master of eloquence, but whose voice, powerful as it was, was every now and then over-borne by its ill-omened screams. The real reason of *his* dreading it indeed was, that he was less a master of thought, than of words. He read his Bible with reverence, indeed he shaped his practice by it; but then, among his consti-tuents, there was a large following who did not. And be-cause they were his constituents, and moreover so many, he considered himself not only bound to abstain from quarrelling with them, but to see likewise that they had their own way. And they said they wanted to have schools in which there should be no Bible taught. There were large constituencies in other parts of the country where the same views were prevalent, and the same wishes ex-pressed. And there was a handful or more of aspirants to distinction on his side of the House, ready to espouse any cause that would give them a name, who now threw them-selves into this, and threatened to desert if they were not heard. Between two such fires it was difficult to remain for any time without being scorched. What was to be done? Was the country ripe for purely secular schools? Would it consent to be taxed for their support? Would it be safe to ask even Parliament to establish schools in which the Bible should be prohibited? "Divide et im-pera," whispered one, who had learnt Machiavelli by heart when he was at college. What it would be impossible for us to do for the nation, there is no saying but what the nation may elect to do for itself. "Italia fara de se" has much to recommend it; why should it not be tried here? Make the British public arbiter of its own fate. Let it have power given to it through its parishes to act as it will. If one sheep hits upon a gap in the hedge, the rest will follow.

Such I take to have been substantially the process by which the Elementary Education Act was arrived at, over and above the thirst, the morbid thirst, on the part of the Liberals in general to win their spurs. Otherwise there was no demand on the part of the country for any fresh scheme. Population was increasing in abnormal proportions; consequently, schools were being everywhere required in greater number, and at a much quicker rate, than they had hitherto been supplied. But the machinery which existed was all in good working order, and had only to be doubled or trebled to meet the want. A word from Government, accompanied with a promise of additional aid, would have sufficed to put all religious bodies on their mettle; and by stimulating private munificence, would have secured the increase required at half the public cost. Nobody was any longer favoured or privileged; nobody could complain that his neighbours received assistance beyond their exertions, or that he was not seconded himself in exact proportion to his own diligence. Nonconformists, indeed, were beginning to complain, and I am disposed to think with some reason, that the Church of England, owing to her vantage-ground, received more than her due. Still, a general measure was not needed to adjust what was in fact a money claim. Even the religious difficulty had been tided over successfully. The conscience-clause protected all who appealed to it for relief; and, side by side with its attempering influence, there were symptoms of a spontaneous re-action on the part of the clergy from the narrow views which had caused it to be passed. I myself always held the opinion that instruction in the Church Catechism should be given in church, not in school, and to candidates for Confirmation, not to the very young. Much as I esteem it, I have seen a dozen catechisms at least of late years, that I should prefer for the very young, even in church. But in school I was always against teaching anything beyond the Creed, the Lord's Prayer, and the Ten Commandments, besides the Bible. What Non-conformist would ever have pressed for a conscience-clause, had this been done? Persons, again, are becoming more rational about the Church Catechism, and even the Prayer-book, than they used to be. Talk of them both in comparison with the Bible! Why, neither of them are three hundred years old as yet; neither of them are used in any country but this; and both of them have been changed, and might be changed again. Besides, is it not their chief merit, that they have been drawn from the Bible? Look at the Bible from this point of view. I will undertake to say that all the books in existence put together have not contributed half so much towards moulding our national character, towards making Englishmen what they are, and have been for centuries, as this one. Part of it is the oldest written record in the world extant. All Christians, all the world over, accept it with reverence just as it stands now, just as it has stood for eighteen centuries, and appeal to it as their written law. Judges may differ about its interpretation, but all uphold it, all subscribe to it, all defer to it in their judgments. In its English dress it is a model of style. But the other day, a time-honoured veteran in the Liberal ranks said of it, "that you might as well teach Greek without Homer, as English without the Bible." Consequently, there is no other book in our language capable of being taught so well, or of serving better as a general medium of instruction for all classes in our parochial schools. A child learns his religion in it and his mother tongue simultaneously, both in their purest forms. There are parts of it which he can understand as soon as he can lisp; and there are parts of it which unfold themselves to him day by day as he grows older; and there are parts of it which he ponders over and over again to his dying day with increased interest, without ever being able to fathom quite. Its stories, its proverbs, its prophecies, its parables, its prayers, its praises, its rules of life, fix themselves one by one in his memory, never to be displaced by anything he may acquire subsequently, and become his cherished companions through life.   If he has any heart at all, there is One Character in it on which the oftener he gazes he feels a glow steal over him, and a desire to improve morally; till, out of pure love, he ends by being won over not merely to become a candidate for heaven, but a better citizen, a more profitable member of society, by contemplating It.

What adequate reason was given, or could have been given, for unsettling the unique supremacy which this superlative book had won for itself, and was still holding, with infinite benefit alike to parents and children, to teachers and pupils in English schools and in English homes? Not certainly that it was incapable of being used without bias for instructing the young in the precepts and practices of the Gospel *sufficiently to ensure their turning out good citizens,* which was all that the State could want, and which was precisely just what had never been attempted hitherto.   If any change there was to be, why should it not have been tried, at all events, in this direction first?

Hitherto, the conditions of the educational grant had been; 1. That it was applied to assist existing schools; 2. That it had never assisted any schools in which religion was not taught; 3. That it assisted all schools in which religion was taught on equal terms, leaving them free to teach it in their own way.   In the Debates on Elementary Education in 1870, it was allowed again and again, that there were practically no schools in this country where religion was not taught in some form or other; in any case, that there were no purely secular schools then receiving aid from the State.   Thus the State was at that time committed to a system of education of the most approved kind; if not practically requiring, at least practically securing all the advantages of a Christian education for all its children; effectuating their being brought up in the way best calculated, humanly speaking, to make them good men and good citizens in mature life. What it said virtually to the Denominations, was this : "As long as the education given in your schools is conducted on Christian principles, and instructs children in the precepts and practices of the Gospel, I am content to leave the subject of dogma free. You may teach them, in addition, as few or as many doctrines as you think fit; use what books you will; interpret Scripture, for that matter, after your own fashion. I shall confine myself to seeing that religion is taught, and as efficiently taught as anything else. Your children will, accordingly, be examined in it by my inspectors, as a general rule; but simply with a view of testing their knowledge of the books they have learnt in school; and with no reference to doctrine whatever as such. If a parent should object to any doctrinal book used in the school to which his child goes, his child is dispensed from learning or being examined in it by a conscience clause."

It was admitted on all hands, that this plan, *as a whole,* gave general satisfaction; at all events, that the country was unanimous in electing to maintain it *in principle.* " We have no doubt whatever," said the mover of the Bill, " that an enormous majority of this country prefer that there should be a Christian training for their children ; that they should be taught to read the Bible." He announced in the strongest terms his own unconquerable repugnance to a national system of secular education. He quoted with undisguised enthusiasm a testimony to the merits of "the Saxon Bible," which, though penned in bitterness, could not be surpassed for homage. "But then," he added, "it would not be for us to prescribe that the Bible must be taught." *Not for us*—not for the Government, I presume, the right hon. Gentleman meant. But, if so, what, in the name of all that is sacred, were they there for ? If people who accept the responsibilities of governing a State, have neither the courage to prescribe what would be for its good; nor [to resist legalizing what would be for its harm; what, indeed, are they there for? Is it the part of a statesman to say, " I denounce suicide myself as a crime, but I have no objection to pass a law leaving everybody free to commit it or not, as he will."

If the State was to have schools of its own, was it not to educate *for itself* in the first place? was it to be satisfied that any system of education, short of the best, for manufacturing good citizens, should be pursued in its schools? If secular education alone was insufficient for that purpose, was it to be left to the school-board of any locality—metropolitan or otherwise—to say whether they would allow more? Was not this an Imperial question of the first order, to be decided only by Parliament? and was Parliament to be deterred from making religious instruction for children between the ages of five and thirteen, imperative, merely because there are numerous points in speculative religion, on which full-grown men squabble? As well might Parliament be deterred from passing any more laws, because judges and jurisconsults, to say nothing of ordinary mortals, are frequently by the ears about their meaning. Accordingly, the seventh clause should have decided that point for all schools alike, by prescribing unequivocally, that in every elementary school, being a public elementary school within the meaning of the Act, the Bible should be used for instructing children in their duties to God and man; and that children should be regularly examined in the same on those points whenever they were examined on other subjects. Then the fourteenth clause, instead of *proscribing* Catechisms, &c., for board-schools, should have *prescribed* the Creed, the Lord's Prayer, and the Ten Commandments for general use, as comprising what the State required that every child should be taught on public grounds. The lack of moral courage which every collision between principle and party reveals in our leading statesman is one of the worst signs of our times. Was not this, in reality, the sort of measure for which the country was prepared, for which all would have been grateful but a very few? and would it not have been in exact harmony with the course which the State had pursued hitherto?

"I understand," said the now Prime Minister, "it is agreed on both sides of the House, that we are to recognise the determination of the great majority of the people of this country, that a national education is to be a religious education. I understand that is the admission of those who are avowedly, and no doubt conscientiously, advocates of a secular education." Nobody denied this, nobody maintained this more strongly than the mover of the Bill himself, as I have before shewn in his own words. Yet he not only shrank from affirming anything of this kind in his Bill, but actually modified it in committee for party purposes, as though his countrymen had changed their mind: actually put power into their hands to do for their children what he himself admitted was opposed to their convictions of right and wrong, and to his own into the bargain. His Bill, instead of being entitled, "An Act to provide for public elementary education in England and Wales," will be known hereafter as " *the* Act for effectually discouraging religious instruction everywhere." This is what lurks in every clause where it is not expressed; this is what is never expressed but in negatives, lest its cloven *animus* should betray itself. Look at its conscience clause, which is said to have been framed with so much care. Of course it has; so much so, that we shall do best to go, for its real import, to one who may be fairly credited with having peeped behind the scenes: "You tell us on the one hand," said Mr., now Sir Vernon Harcourt, "that religion is the basis of all education; and we accept that statement, and establish religious schools. You say it is the greatest and most important part of education; and then you give effect to your declaration, by telling the children when they come to school, 'You must not fail to attend to reading, writing, arithmetic, and geography; but there is one subject you may entirely neglect if you please : when religion is about to be imparted, you may go and play at marbles in the gutter.' This is the conscience clause."

The Conscience Clause—to the eternal disgrace, be it said, of those who framed it — framed in the name of liberty to inveigle and then enslave hand and foot, principles and practice, those that had till then been free! What were the champions of schools founded or supported by private munificence for Christian ends doing, when they allowed it to be made, without protest, a condition of any further aid from the State, that they should in future consent to have the manner of their religious instruction so arranged for them, as to present religion in the guise of a thing taught on sufferance, in the twilight before or after regular school hours : which teachers were to be discouraged from explaining lest they should trench upon dogma ; and pupils from learning, as it no longer counted among the subjects of their examination : which every incentive to teach well was studiously cancelled, and every facility to learn ill, or not at all, multiplied, as though it conferred exemption from bondage? And all this, on the assumption that people were too blind to detect in it a sop to the secularists; too dense to divine, that when anything which had once formed a subject for examination is ordered to be examined in no longer, it is because it is *meant* to be shelved !

Then, finally, while church-schools even are compelled, under pain of forfeiting their grants, to teach religion from henceforth in this hole-and-corner fashion, to the lowering it in the eyes of teachers and pupils alike ; one schoolboard after another may forsooth, at their discretion, not only forbid its being taught at all in theirs, but compel children, whose parents can afford them no better education, to attend schools, in which there is neither any religious observance nor instruction allowed, or fine the parents for their non-attendance. For, " ought we to restrict school-boards in regard to religion more than we do the managers of voluntary schools? We have come to the conclusion that we ought not—" said the mover of this Bill. Double-distilled hypocrite! I should have said; had I not been convinced from his habitually frank speech at other times, that in this case it was a mere slip of the tongue. But what *can* he mean? They bind one, who is solemnly bound to teach religion, to submit to teach it in the degrading and offensive way already described; they bind the other, who is under no obligations of any sort, to nothing whatever, except to teach it or not, as he will. And this they call justice! Thus the school-boards are given by law a despotic power infinitely more oppressive than the old Conscience Clause was designed to correct in the clergy. For though the clergy could, before that Conscience Clause was passed, compel every child attending their schools to learn the Church Catechism, they could compel no parent to send his child to their schools; the school-boards, on the contrary, may first decree that there shall be no religious teaching of any kind in their schools, and then fine every parent whose children, being of the legal age, and unprovided with better education, fail to attend them. The Conscience Clause was passed to prevent the clergyman of a parish influencing children to become Churchmen; the Elementary Education Act sanctions the school-board influencing children to become Pagans.

To such straits have the dearest liberties of the subject been reduced, under a Liberal Government pandering to demagogues and secularists. I suppose greater iniquity was never veiled under the sanction of law. I say it is injustice that would justify revolt against law, if it could be redressed by no other means. Birmingham has, with unenviable notoriety, taken the lead in excluding religion from her board-schools, and making the education given in them purely secular. If I lived in Birmingham, I would go to prison five times a-day sooner than submit to pay a fine for not sending my children to schools where they were forbidden to be taught religion, at the dictation of any school-board whatsoever; and I would make common cause with the poorest, threatened to be similarly tyrannized over. Moreover, I would resist being rated for the support of any such schools, at Birmingham or elsewhere. I am a peaceable, law-loving subject in general; but I hold that everybody would be justified in resisting any scheme for unchristianizing his country by every means in his power. The minister who would interpose between the rising generation and this unnatural, anti-christian, unrighteous, suicidal Act for miseducating them, would deserve the thanks of his country better than he who saved it from the first Napoleon.

———————♦———————

Printed by James Parker and Co., Crown-yard, Oxford.